Before getting started, your author wants to make it clear that you've opened the book of 'Spiritual Straight Talk' that's promoting only, *independently*, the character of God, the kind of person He is, **and not linked to any religion or spiritual group.**

Are you about to shout

STOP

THE WORLD

I WANT TO GET OFF?

IF SO

For those of you willing to **listen**

discover ahead

SOLID evidence for understanding

all the craziness

along with

The big **WHY** question

WHY

If there is a loving God

Then why all the
Pain, suffering, and death?

By

Edward R. Sager

Why

If there is a loving God

Then why all the

Pain, suffering, and death?

Copyright © 2018 by Edward R. Sager

Revised again – March 2022

ISBN-13: 978-1-9831-9276-0

World rights reserved. This book or any portion thereof may not be copied or reproduced in any form or manner whatever, except as provided by law, without the written permission of the publisher, except by reviewer who may quote brief passages in a review.

The author assumes full responsibility for the accuracy of all facts and quotations as cited in this book.

PAST REVIEWS

Your author, after 40 years of study within the subject, is convinced that Revelation 12 is correct about the WHOLE world being led astray – led astray about the kind of person God is.

Which should lead to the understanding that God is NOT as most promote Him to be.

"Love and obey me, or be torture in Hell – REALLY, are you sure about that?"

In the past, many have said that my picture of God is awesome, it makes us think.

While others, mainly pastors have said, "your writings are only going to confuse people."

After your journey through this short three hour read, please report your review; have you been enlightened or totally confused?   *(0 to 5)*

Dedication & Introduction

This book is dedicated to all who are mystified or puzzled with the BIG WHY question. Why is it that bad things happen to good people?

My perspective is centered on the kind of God I've been shown Him to be, along with *how* God is revealing the ways of Lucifer, now known as the Devil.

You'll soon discover why the BIG WHY question is alive and well, is because most people don't know the God that's described in this publication.

For most teach Him to be, what He is NOT.

In other words, knowing the God described within, is essential to having the peace that causes understanding to happen, with the BIG WHY question.

In viewing the evidence ahead of what God is like, you could be found in a state of denial, or ecstatically excited about promoting the same God that Jesus came to reveal.

In fact, to know the true God that Jesus came to reveal, is to know perfect freedom, away from the many deceptive diversions about the character of God, exposed ahead.

To begin with, you'll find some basic history of what happened in the control center of the universe, that some of us call Heaven.

This is where rebellion against God began, with Lucifer, and not with of Adam and Eve, here on earth.

With that understanding, many avenues of enlightenment can come into view within the BIG WHY question.

Remarkable avenues, including a *WHY* that's not a question, but maybe even a bigger why, of **WHY Jesus came to earth**.

You'll soon discover that Jesus came with outstanding good news, that should have transformed the most spiritual folk of his day, but instead, they crucified him.

Yes, Jesus came with a better and more believable good news gospel, that you'll also soon discover, is still being ignored. (2022)

Biblical history has informed us that the Devil has been roaming the earth from the beginning of time, distorting the true picture of God.

His distortions have taken the path of presenting God as an executioner, threatening those that refuse to love and obey Him in a torturing place of Hell.

Some say it's our choice to pick where we want to spend eternity – in Heaven or Hell.

But since God is the creator of all things – to have created a torturing place for those that refuse Him – sounds more like the Devil's picture of God, than anything else – especially after reviewing the outstanding evidence ahead.

With the BIG WHY question centered on a God that has the power to end it, but doesn't, surely suggest that there is far more to it than what's currently being taught.

For those of you that believe Jesus came primarily to save us from the wrath of an offended God, I must ask a question.

Is it possible for you to be open, open enough to listen to the words of Jesus, where he states a different reason for his coming?

I sincerely believe you'll be pleasantly surprised for allowing his words to soak in.

For God sent Jesus with a special message that the Devil has been totally successful, so far, in covering up, with a false picture of God.

His results have people, the world around deceived and confused, confused enough to be wondering why God is allowing all the pain, suffering, and death.

The history of this world should convince us that Revelation 12:9 is right, in stating that the whole world will be lead astray, deceived about the kind of person God is.

For many ascribe to the concept that God made a perfect world and we humans messed it up by sinning, therefore, causing God to be angry enough to punish us sinners with all kinds of pain, suffering, and death.

This picture of God has been conjured-up by the Devil, as he thinks God to be unfair with him, for being cast out of Heaven, down to this earth.

With the understanding that God gave him a place to show us his stuff, how his ways are, supposedly, better than God's — says volumes about the wisdom of God.

For God's strategy is about revealing to us, just how clever the Devil has been in distorting the good news of the gospel into, what it is NOT.

As said before, Jesus came with different good news, far better and more believable good news, than what is currently being taught.

In completing your journey through this publication, more than likely, you'll be wondering why some of the most spiritual are continuing to refuse the words from

Jesus, the same as way back then, when they crucified him.

After listening to the words of Jesus, you'll discover a picture of God that deserves our respect, as He is respectful of our free will choices.

You'll also discover a God that is far from any kind of threat in coercing anyone with pain, suffering, and death.

You'll discover how the Devil has placed God down to our level by twisting spiritual lingo into threats of punishment, and death — instead of a warning against going outside of the way God made us to function.

Discover how the diversion of busyness, the busyness of forever working on our good behavior has got in the way of learning more about the God that Jesus came to reveal.

This was designed by the enemy to cover up the real issue of why Jesus came to earth.

You'll also discover that this sin thing – a breach of trust in God – is what changes people - people continuing down the path of irresponsible behavior will eventually experience the fact that sin, **not God**, pays its own wage, which is pain, suffering, and death.

If you will stay with me to the end – you'll discover how you can have a part in bringing an end to all the pain, suffering, and death.

In listening to the words of Jesus, you'll soon discover that he came to reveal his Father as a God of peace, a God of kindness, a God of forgiveness, and unconditional love for all.

Come, let us reason together

If we could become unified in who God is

WOW! --- That would be outstanding!

Note: Because of the importance of what's ahead, parts of this may sound, somewhat, redundant – maybe because a certain issue has yet to soak in.

But giving time to digest it, it could become beautiful music to your ears.

Something like the little girl asking her Mommy to read it again, for the best of the best is the good news that Jesus came to proclaim –

"Please Mommy, read it again."

Content

Part 1 – (Page 17) of this book is packed with thought provoking evidence for what it means to know God.

You'll discover it to be far more important to learn all we can about God the Father – far more important than spending most of our time on trying to please a God, we may not know. For knowing God is life eternal – John 17:3

You'll also discover a ***different good news gospel*** straight from the words of Jesus, giving us a different perspective in why there is no other way to Heaven but through Jesus and the message Jesus came to deliver or proclaim.

Hopefully, you'll discover reasons for digging like digging for hidden treasure, in what it really means to know God.

Part 2 – (Page 64) of this book is an amazing conversation with God, a conversation that again, hopefully will answer 'thee-all famous' question of WHY.   (**Also see a Short Summary** – Page 93)

PART 1

Hey, you wonderfully made God created people out there, with all the craziness going on throughout the world; shouldn't it be time for some answers to the big **why** – along with why we are even here?

These questions have been worked on by many for centuries, possibly one of the reasons why there are so many different religions, or spiritual groups.

As stated in the beginning, your author wants to make it clear that this little book is promoting only the character of God, the kind of person He is, and not any religion.

Also, to express much respect for those of you laboring to bring people to a knowledge of God.

Although, being sensitive to everyone's belief system, my plea to everyone, is to notice a gracious God, a picture of a God that weeps over anyone that would refuse Him. A God that would say, - "Oh, how can I give you up, how can I let you go, my heart winces within; my compassion grows warm and tender. <u>I won't act on the heat of anger,</u> for I am God and not a human being." (Hosea 11)

Notice a God that forces no one with anger or threats of pain, suffering, and death.

With all the questions, and different pictures of God being alive and well, is it any wonder that the world is full of Atheists and Skeptics along with many other ways to describe those that are struggling with the concept of there even being a God?

I believe this boils down to many thinking people, struggling to make sense of all the craziness, for even spiritual things must make sense – 2+2 must add up to 4 - or we might be led to believe in fairy tales.

If it wasn't for what I've been shown over the past 40 years, more than likely one of those skeptic labels would be on me.

Although sympathizing with those questioning if God even exists, I could never let go of thinking about the wonder of God, especially after considering the awesome workings of the human body as well as looking through the lens of the Hubble Telescope. The evidence for intelligent design far outweighs the different concepts that try to leave God out of the picture.

I concluded that with a loving and gracious God in over-all control, He must have a very significant reason for allowing all the NUT stuff.

By the way, I'm Ed Sager – a cabinetmaker by trade and founder of 'TimeToThink.us' with thought provoking Spiritual Straight Talk about God - the same Father God that Jesus came to reveal.

The focus of this SPIRITUAL STRAIGHT TALK begins at the beginning with the biblical story of Lucifer's fall from Heaven instead of Adam and Eve's fall, here on earth.

Thoughts of superiority and rebellion against God began there, with God's lead angel, Lucifer, right within the *Heavenly Control Center*.

The Bible records that Lucifer wanted to be like the highest, wanting to be the king, which suggests that God had a political problem on his hands. (Isaiah 14:12-14)

It's revealed that Lucifer went so far as campaigning his erroneous political views throughout the universe, being successful enough to deceive about one third of the brilliant heavenly angles.

Notice that God didn't stop him. What better way for God to reveal the evilness of Lucifers ways than to allow him the time and space to demonstrate his views.

The concept that the Devil was given the opportunity to demonstrate his, so-called better ways, should be a wake-up call to all of us to see the rightness or righteousness of God's ways.

Within God's strategy, He has allowed us to view good against evil, giving us the time and space to view the evidence.

Evidence, which to some of us, reveals a **universe wide** controversy over the character of God, better known as "The Great Controversy."

Some would tone down or weaken this term by stating it as a controversy between good and evil – but make no mistake – with some of the angels being involved, ***it's a <u>universe wide</u> controversy over the kind of God He is.***

With spiritual issues being over the trustworthiness of God, where about one third of the brilliant angels were turned against Him, <u>notice ahead the methods</u> God used to clear up the confusion.

GOD'S STRATEGIC METHODS

1. To reveal that rebellion against God, began with Lucifer in the heavenly control center, and not here on earth, with Adam and Eve.
2. To create earth, the Devil's sandbox, where Lucifer / the Devil, 'the great

deceiver' has been roaming from the beginning of time.

3. To allow Lucifer to show us his stuff – by deceiving the whole world (Rev. 12) into believing a false picture of God.
4. To reveal how this false picture reached an extreme level, before Jesus was sent to offset or refute the lie's he had spread throughout the _universe_, about God.
5. To reveal how the **most spiritual people** of the day found reason to crucify him, in him threatening their flow of income by revealing the Father as being just like him.
6. To reveal how subtly the Devil has worked in twisting certain biblical issues, making it sound acceptable for God to be an extortionist, in requiring a blood sacrifice, before He would grant forgiveness.

With this little dab of biblical history, hopefully, you'll catch the picture of God's purpose for this world. A place to allow evil to run its course, to the point of revealing to each of us, how wrong evil really is.

This is God's strategy to secure the universe against evil ever happening again. For each of us needs to be convinced, in our own mind, that God ways are right.

Surely it makes sense that the Creator of this vast universe would have a fool proof strategy to clear up the confusion about Himself.

Even to the point of allowing the Devil to paint a false picture of Him throughout the universe.

< --- >

What's ahead was hard to put into words – in fact, writers have a symbolic term of 'hitting a wall' – my body did not hit a wall – but my mind, surely did.

Struggling for days over how to write this, that it's not taken as a threat to anyone's salvation. But instead, hopefully it's taken as outstanding good news about God.

By the way, the words – Lucifer, Satan, or the Devil throughout this book are synonymous, meaning the same person.

Biblical issues listed in sequence, are KEY points in understanding how the spiritual world has been led astray, just as Revelation 12:9 describes.

1. A universe wide issue ------------- 27
2. God's timing ----------------------- 32
3. In legal trouble --------------------- 34
4. The Misuse of Two Texts --------- 36
5. The ignoring of Genesis 3:4 ------ 38
6. The Misuse of John 3:16 ---------- 44
7. Every Word – REALLY? ------------ 46
8. Word meaning changes ----------- 49
9. Symbolic meanings ---------------- 51
10.   Being Forgiven or Healed -- 54
11.   The Good News ---------------57

The *meanings* behind these few biblical issues, has much to do with our understanding of the BIG WHY question, which must include our picture of God.

(Maybe good to fasten seatbelt here)

1 – A universe wide issue

In the beginning of this publication, it was told of Lucifer, now known as the Devil, being cast out of Heaven – why - what was the **issue**? Revelation 12:7 states that WAR broke out in heaven. Again, why, what was the **issue**?

Our texts, (Rev.12) also states that the Devil has led the whole world astray - has led the whole world astray about what? What is or was the issue?

Again, earlier in this publication it was told that many ascribe to the concept that God made a perfect world and we humans messed it up by sinning. It's been assumed that this made God angry – but this concept can't be further from the truth.

It's been the Devil's business to fabricate the false gospel, making God out to be vengeful, unforgiven, and severe, which if scrutinized, is the foundation under the now taught legal plan of salvation. *(2022)*

The concept of God requiring a blood sacrifice before granting forgiveness was carried out in ancient biblical history – even to the extent of people sacrificing their own children on the alter.

It shouldn't be a surprise for the Devil to have carried this same concept into our modern-day beliefs of God requiring the better blood of Jesus before granting forgiveness.

Hopefully, after viewing the evidence ahead the absurdity of such beliefs will become ridiculous.

Of course, God is disappointed, with His children for not listening – but angry - really?

Romans 1 describes God's anger against all ungodly behavior.

Read it for yourself; "because they refused to listen, God let them go to their own rebellious choices." More than likely, crying as He walked away.

No, the issue is not over God being angry with us for sinning, for the real issue is far larger than that.

Consider the biblical fact, with about one third of the brilliant heavenly angles being deceived too, that the larger issue is a **universe wide issue** over what God is like, the kind of person God is.

Also, to be considered, is when Jesus came to earth with this message, the most spiritual folk of the day crucified him – they had to get rid of him because his message was affecting their flow of income from the people. (See more ahead - from page 85 - 87)

The Devil, without a doubt, has made the **issue** to be about us gaining forgiveness from our bad behavior. The concept of Jesus taking our place in the death we allegedly deserve, has been taught as our solution for being saved.

But when listening to Jesus, Jesus alone, you'll soon discover, his words do NOT support that.

Jesus came with far better good news, in that the Father is just like him – the message he came to proclaim.

This is the ISSUE above all ISSUES!

That God is NOT as most describe Him

to be.

What's immediately ahead is undeniable evidence in revealing how crafty the Devil has been in his business of adding and twisting words to distort the ways of God – making God out to be what He is NOT.

It should prove to be very enlightening to most levels of understanding about how the Devil has covered up the GOOD NEWS that Jesus came to proclaim about his Father.

2 - GOD'S TIMING

Beginning with 2nd Timothy 2:15 – "To rightly divide the word of truth."

In rightly dividing the Word, the apostle Paul warns about arguing over words, using big words to confuse the truth about God.

It's evidence, that must be considered to prove the true picture of God, the same Father God that Jesus came to reveal.

The design is meant to promote thinking, to think before leaping, think to see the error with what we may have thought to be truth.

For God to allow the Devil to deceive some of the angels, should speak volumes to God's methods in revealing truth to each one of us.

Another thought in rightly dividing truth within our spiritual journey, is to notice that God, just might, just might have a specific time for certain spiritual things to be exposed.

Because of what's happening around the world, Titus 1:3 could be interpreted for now, for it states that - at an appointed time, some spiritual things will be brought to light.

To add more (John 16:12) Jesus said he had much more to tell us, but he held back, for we were not ready to handle it at the time.

Could it be said that maybe the time is now?

We all should know that knowledge for most everything in life has increased – so, why not consider that spiritual knowledge has increased as well?

3 - In Legal Trouble?

The Devil has been successful *(within the currently taught, plan of salvation)* in leading the whole world astray in twisting many biblical meanings within the concept of us being in legal trouble with God.

It all began after the Devil deceived Eve into eating the forbidden fruit – Eve breaking the rules. (Genesis 3)

The Devil then turned the breaking of the rules into a legal problem – but more than that, he promoted the concept that God became angry about His rules being broken.

This has turned the mission of Jesus into dying on the cross to pay the price for sinning or to satisfy certain legal demands from the Father. Legal demands conjure-up by the Devil that doesn't exist– for that concept is the Devil's evil scheming strategy against God.

Instead of being in legal trouble, you'll soon discover that Jesus came, primarily, to reveal the true God of Heaven to us, by demonstrating God's kindness.

"For don't you know it's God's kindness that leads us to repentance?"

(See Romans 2:4)

Did you get that? It's God's kindness that leads us sinners to repentance.

4 – The Misuse of Two Texts
Romans 6:23 & Genesis 3:3

The legal concept, within the currently taught plan of salvation, surely came from the _misuse_ of these two famous texts, given by biblical scholars for centuries to prove that God is the executioner in the consequence of death for sin. *(The wages of sin is death – and you must not touch it, or you will surely die.)*

These two statements have been assumed as a legal death sentence from God, assumed, because the texts don't say how we would die or who would kill us.

In rightly dividing Scripture, these texts are not a death sentence from God, but instead, they are warnings from God.

Warnings against going down roads of sinful, irresponsible behavior.

The CEB (Common English Bible) translation states that *sin* will pay the wage of death - for sin pays its own wage - because sin of itself, is a deadly cancer.

Of course, the wage of sin is death – there is no question about it. To continue down wrong roads of behavior will end in – death.

But not at the hands of God.

Assuming God to be the executioner, doesn't make it true.

Just more evidence in how the Devil has deceived the whole world into believing a false picture of who God is.

For what kind of God would He be to say, "love and obey me, or I'll kill you?

5 - The Misuse of Genesis 3:4

We must come to grips with the fact that the Devil has been alive and well from the beginning of time, doing everything he can to distort the ways of God. One of which is found in Genesis 3:4 where the Devil is found lying to Eve that she would not surely die.

There has to be something drastically wrong here, when the whole world seems to be following the Devil's lie, in promoting the concept that we have been made as eternal beings – never dying.

Especially, after 1st Timothy 6:16 states that only God is immortal, along with Ecclesiastes 9 - about the dead knowing nothing.

However, there is outstanding good news within 1st Corinthians 15:51-55 where it states that immorality *(never dying)* occurs at the second coming of Jesus.

The huge fraud coming from biblical scholars for centuries in insinuating we've been made as eternal beings, inspired the concept of a forever burning Hell, when they realized that God would need a place for those that refused Him.

This is also where the fear-based gospel came from, centered on a down-under, place of Hell.

Fortunately, the hard facts in the Bible don't support a never dying or a torturing down-under place of Hell.

However, the concept has proven to be a good scare tactic that has turned many away from evil.

In fact, in a close personal experience, I had a scoundrel of an uncle, that my mother told me was so crooked, he couldn't lay in bed straight. (LOL)

But one day his son talked him into going to an evangelistic meeting where the sermon was on the burning in Hell message. With tears streaming down my uncle's face, he got up, walked to the front, and gave his heart to the God.

Whatever it takes, is OK with me – praise God for his scare tactics!

As you can see, there is a specific reason, a godly reason, for the torturing in Hell concept.

It's changed lives that would have never turned from evil any other way. The same as in the Bible story of Jonah.

Like I said, a good scare tactic, but where did this concept of a *down-under* place come from – is it real?

What and where is Hell?

The Old Testament lists Hell 31 times as "Shelo," which means "the grave." In the New Testament, 10 times as "Hades," which means "the grave," 12 times as "Gehenna," which means "the place of burning," and 1 time as "Tartarus," a place of darkness. A total of 54 times with all these different meanings.

It appears we don't have to look deep to realize that all the above descriptions of Hell fit the very world, we are living in.

It's obvious that we are living in a world that was made to reveal the Devil's ways - where the results are - pain, suffering, and death.

This subject is so important within the Big Why question, I've dedicated chapter 13 in **"An Awakening"** to the subject.

It's packed with far more detail.

God's methods, like in the Bible story of Jonah, has been allowed to function around a 'Fear Based Gospel' – straighten up and fly right or be destroyed. *(Or be tortured in Hell)*

For the benefit of saving some.

Many assume that the Bible story, the Rich Man and Lazarus, (Luke 16: 19-31) is proof of a down-under place of Hell.

But if taken to the end of the story, it's obvious that the story is a parable, not reality – saying, "If they do not listen to Moses and the Prophets they will not be convinced, *(convinced to turn from their wicked ways)* even if someone rises from the dead."

Your author has never believed there is a down-under place of Hell – unless it's a down-under place from Heaven called earth.

But I sincerely believe that God has a purpose in the use of scare tactics, as in the book of Jonah.

SCARE TACTICS – REALLY?

Yes, really!

For I hear God saying in Jonah 4:11 - "Shouldn't I have concern for the many thousands of scoundrels in the world, that may not turn from evil, any other way?"

6 - Misuse of John 3:16

With the fear based, legal concepts of God's requirements being alive and well, it set the stage for many legal minds to work on many different and complicated ways to convince God to grant us forgiveness.

The legal concept became convincing and acceptable to the people after John 3:16 introduced a **loving** Father for sending Jesus to die a legal death sentence, in our place.

But shocking as it should be, the texts doesn't say that Jesus came to die in our place – again, it's only been assumed.

Paraphrased: What our famous texts really says, one must include going on to verse 19 – where it states that Jesus came as a <u>LIGHT to the world</u> – that whosoever believeth in the good news message that Jesus came to give (the good news about his Father) would be everlasting life to them.

Allowing the concept of Jesus coming as a light to the world, to **soak in,** has everything to do with understanding the real reason for why Jesus came to save us.

Jesus came to save us from the lies that have infiltrated the whole world about his Father.

He came to reveal that his Father is just like him, full of compassion and unconditional love for all.

7 - Every Word – REALLY?

This next one, 2nd Timothy 3:16 has been preached around the world, from most every pulpit under the sun, that all Scripture is infallible, that **every word** is God breathed.

But in the original 'KJV' (King James Version) before the little italicized word - *IS* – was added, it read that every *inspired* word is God breathed – not every word – *IS*.

Simply add a little common sense - to see the impossibility of every word being from God, with many twisted meanings of words within hundreds of different translations.

Even the thought of the original being the ONE – is questionable with the influence of the Devil roaming the earth from the beginning of time.

Again, adding a word and assuming it to be true, doesn't make it true.

Even more reason to be listening to the words of Jesus alone, instead of other sources.

Adding to that, just because it's in 'Red Letter form' *(assumed words from Jesus)* but seemingly out of character for God – should be compared with how subtle the Devil has been in twisting certain words to fit his agenda. Simply weigh all things against what is being revealed here, about the true character of God.

Listening to other sources, instead of Jesus has served the Devil's agenda very well, in getting every 'spiritual group' under the sun into mass confusion over the picture of God.

By adding words and changing the meaning of certain words is how the enemy has worked in his endeavors to make God out to be vengeful, unforgiving, and severe.

This is how the legal view against the great controversy view of the cross has taken the world by storm, by changing & manipulating certain words.

> *There's evidence galore to this fact in chapter 16 of "The Gig is Up – The Charade is Over" – found by clicking "View Books" in TimeToThink.us.*

It may be a hard pill to swallow for many, to think that God would allow our precious Bibles to be tampered with, but never forget, within God's strategy, He allowed about one third of the brilliant heavenly angels to be deceived.

So, what makes us think we haven't been deceived as well, for – possibly - the same reason.

8 - Word Meaning Changes

This next one, 'changing the meaning', has had huge effects in turning the picture of God, into what He is NOT.

Our word to examine is ATONEMENT.

The original meaning of atonement is found in the multivolume set of the Oxford English Dictionary, where it states, "in the thirteenth century it meant being at one, being in harmony with."

Many years later the word was being used as an "appeasement, making amends, paying the penalty to satisfy legal demands.

The Oxford English goes on the say, "Here the idea of reconciliation or reunion is practically lost sight of under that of legal satisfaction or amends."

As you can see, with the enemy being alive and well, he has distorted the meaning of atonement (AT-ONE-MENT) over to God needing to be appeased with the blood of Jesus before He would grant forgiveness.

A distortion of God's character like no other.

This switch in meaning, should alone prove to be undeniable evidence that the Bible has been tampered with, making it appear as though God needed to be appeased with the better blood of Jesus before granting forgiveness. (Shocking)

9 - Symbolic Meanings

In this next one, we Christians sing, "Nothing but the blood of Jesus" – but we must ask, what does that mean?

Recorded in John 6, Jesus is saying "he that eateth my flesh, and drinketh my blood, hath eternal life; and I will raise him up at the last day. (KJV) Again, we must ask for the meaning.

For sure – strange and symbolic terms – for no one actually eats his flesh and drinks his blood, but symbolically, his flesh and blood represent his life, even his way of life, to be digested – or to become AT-ONE or in harmony with.

Most of us have heard the symbolic term that *'we are what we eat'* – Jesus was simply saying, feed on me, feed on the words I have given you – if you do, my words will become a part of you - you will become like the one you most admire.

In the song, "nothing but the blood of Jesus" – symbolically means to - "follow nothing but the _life_ of Jesus" – rather than thinking that the blood of Jesus has some magical ingredient that has something to do with gaining forgiveness from the Father.

Many of us grew from childhood believing that the blood of Jesus covered over our smelling, filthy rages of sin – that the Father only sees us through the perfect life of Jesus.

That concept may be a warm, fussy feeling for many – but it leaves out the fact that God the Father surely has 20/20 vision to see us as we are.

The real good news in the gospel is that God sees us as we are, and still loves us!!! It's only the Devil that's insinuating that God can't stand filthy, sinful human beings.

For more back-up in the dynamics of the good news about the Father, is again, within the words of Jesus, found in the prodigal son story.

If we were to look closely, we might see tears of joy streaming down the face of the Father, as He is found running to meet us on our way back home – in smelly rages and all.

Another amazing discovery could be - that the Father didn't listen to the son's repentance speech – but instead, He called for a celebration party.

This is what God is really like, surely no one to be afraid of!

10 - Forgiven or Healed

Rightly understood, these symbolic terms about the blood of Jesus are a solid rock of truth in the best way to be healed from evil.

Notice, I didn't say forgiven, but instead, I said to be healed, for to be immersed deep into the ways of God, the ways of God that Jesus came to reveal, is a sure way to healing.

Since the spiritual issue throughout the world seems to be center on forgiveness, instead of being healed from the deadly cancer of sin, I once heard an example to compare.

Being forgiven or being healed?

Some of us have been struck with a painful reason for going to a dentist. Would you be seeking forgiveness for not taking care of your teeth properly or to be healed from what has cause you severe pain?

Again, in the prodigal son story, found in Luke 15, the son came back home with all kinds of stories to persuade his father to forgive him, but he soon found that his father had forgiven him before he had left home.

If legal concerns are still alive and well within you, consider the conversation Jesus had with Nicodemus, found in John 3, about being born again, with a new heart and right spirit.

And especially notice the hope that Psalms 51:10 can give to each one of us, as David cries out for God to create in him a new and pure heart and renew a faithful spirit within him.

No, forgiveness is not the issue, but to be healed from the results of sin, surely is.

When we stray away from the words of Jesus, Jesus alone, we may not only, pick up on false meanings to things, but we may also think it to be okay to accept changes to some word meanings – changes that have had major affects to what we believe the good news in the gospel to be.

If most everyone could believe in the good news message that Jesus came to proclaim about his Father, **Luke 4:43** - if that could soak-in - it should take the world by storm.

For it **HAS** to be OUTSTANDING better good news that the Father is no one to be afraid of – He is just like Jesus.

11 - The Good News in the Gospel

Last, but not least, listen to Jesus as he describes a different reason for why he was sent – different from what is currently being taught.

In Luke 4:43, Jesus tells us the reason for why he was sent, was to proclaim the good news about his Father's kingdom, or in other words the good news about the kind of God He is.

And in John 17:4-6 Jesus said he had completed the work he was given to do – that of revealing the true God of Heaven to those he was given out of the world.

At the bottom line, if we are interested – *really interested* - in seeing the 2nd coming of Jesus, we must come to the point of listening to what Jesus said about what it's going to take to bring that into a reality.

First off, John 17:3 states that knowing God is life eternal – Jesus also told us how to really know God, was to feed on his words – his words found in Matthew, Mark, Luke, and John.

I recommend beginning with the book of John first, for John was the closest to Jesus.

Secondly, once you've been filled with the messages from Jesus – it's more than likely you'll notice what Jesus said in Matthew 24:14 – that when the good news about what his Father is like, is taken to the world

- WOW -

then the end will come!

With the conditions of this world being what they are – the messages that came through Jesus about his Father – HAS – to be beautiful music to your ears!

Enough to say, "please Mommy", read it again.

However, if you are continuing to _believe_ the Devil's view of God's requirements for being saved, **instead of Jesus coming to clear up the lies about God's character,** you might want to consider replacing Phillip's name with your name in John 14. Phillip was asking Jesus to show them the Father.

This is where Jesus would ask you, "You've been with me all this time, _(teaching and preaching)_ and you don't know me? If you have seen me, you have seen the Father, He is just as loving and forgiving as me."

> Many know Jesus, but the question is –
> do you really know God the Father?

Again, I must be bold, at the risk of offending those that have been told, "IT'S ALL ABOUT JESUS" all about Jesus making it possible to be accepted by the Father – this concept goes against the message Jesus came to give **the message that got him crucified.**

For Jesus said his work was complete after revealing what his Father was like. In other words, I hear Jesus saying, *"that it's NOT all about me, but instead, it's all about my Father."*

If you have missed that, you could be missing the dynamics within the words coming directly from Jesus.

Consider how our emotions from believing certain spiritual things from childhood can put many into a state of denial against *being convinced with solid evidence.*

In going back to the thought that spiritual things must make sense, the same as 2+2 must equal 4 – when our understanding reaches the level of seeing that Jesus dying on the cross was meant to change us – and **not to** convince God the Father to forgive, a new bright light in our understanding, could come into view!

Within the pandemic scare of early 2020, the closing of churches, has surely directed me to a different path of importance.

Spending time in the book of John, John 14:12 simply jumped off the page at me – where Jesus said, *"Verily, verily, I say unto you, those of you who believe in what I've been doing, will do the same, or greater after I'm gone."*

What I heard Jesus telling me, was "Ed, stop the busyness of playing church – it's time for all of us, to get to work in promoting the same message listed in both Luke 4:43 and John 17:4-6 to be taken around the world.

The good news in the gospel is not certain legal maneuvers on how to gain forgiveness from sin – but instead, it's far greater good news that our Father is the Great Physician that loves us the same as Jesus does, again, surely no one to be afraid of.

So, what's it going to take before we get it, before we get our focus off ourselves and our behavior - and on to knowing God?

Are we to be knocked off our donkeys, so to speak, like in the Bible story about Saul, the man supporting the killing of Christians, before he became the apostle Paul?

Working on our behavior should become secondary to working on knowing God, especially after realizing the simplicity of John 17:3 stating that knowing God is life eternal. For knowing God, *just might have something to do with our behavior!*

Again, are you sure you know the God the Jesus came to reveal?

At any rate, it shouldn't be hard to realize that God is working a strategy that could be over our heads to understand, until He is ready to reveal it. Could the timing be now?

Next, consider a conversation with God - designed to stimulate thinking about what our loving heavenly Father is really like.

PART 2

Just Imagine

A conversation with God

Us: God, what happened to your created children — what caused Lucifer, in the perfect environment of Heaven, to develop thoughts of thinking he could run the affairs of the universe better than you?

God: For a short answer — Lucifer broke the proverbial, eleventh Commandment, so to speak, of "Thou Shalt Not Kid thy self" into thinking he could become God.

In this state of mind, it led him to develop a <u>planned strategy of deception</u>, much like the modern-day political warfare of making false accusations against an opponent.

He campaigned throughout the universe and deceived about one third of my created angels by stating false accusations against me.

Us: Really - that must have been a difficult experience for you to lose the respect and loyalty of your much-loved created children. Can you tell us what your thoughts were?

God: This so saddened me, I had Hosea record me as saying, with tears streaming down my cheeks - "how can I give you up, how can I let you go." (Hosea 11)

Also, I had Paul in Romans 1 explain my wrath against all ungodliness, as leaving them to their own heart's desires, for I knew the only way to really win them back was to allow them to experience the devastation of evil; this is sometimes explained as tough love – which has much to do with understanding the BIG WHY, the why of all the pain, suffering, and death that you've been wondering about.

For you to understand more about what is meant by tough love, I created your world with the family setting where you could understand the feeling of unconditional love toward your children as I do for you.

Tough love is most always thought of, at first, as angry punishment for breaking rules. But this couldn't be further from the truth, for unconditional love means there are no conditions of repentance or proper behavior required before forgiveness is granted. In other words, love and forgiveness is always there.

When it's understood that I'm just as kind, loving, and forgiving as Jesus – this is what leads to repentance and proper behavior.

(See Romans 2:4)

This is what Jesus revealed about ME throughout his life that I'm love, and forgiveness personified – it's who I AM.

"Whoever comes to ME, I will not cast out." (John 6:37)

Tough love punishment is designed to turn one away from evil – for I chasten all I love – which is all.

Us: God, this is amazing info! I always thought you were angry, that your main concern was over your rules being broken. Can you tell us more about what your main concerns are?

God: Well, there are many, but at the top of my list is found in John 17:21 where Jesus and I are discussing our desires for you as being AT-ONE with us as we are AT-ONE with each other.

Of course, we are talking about the renewing of your mind set or in other words, your inner thoughts to be forever turned away from evil.

You've been created with free will choice that I'll never take away, therefore it's so important that you realize that you've been made in my image, to function in the atmosphere of love for each other.

But somehow, you seemed to think I'm angry with you for breaking my rules.

It's like you're picturing Jesus as the good guy that's going to save you from my Devine wrath or something.

And this couldn't be further from the truth; because Jesus and I are AT-ONE with each other – we sing off the same page, so to speak – in fact, Jesus said it all in John 14 that if you have seen him, you have seen me, the Father.

I've been telling you that my love for you is unconditional - I love you the same as Jesus does. Our intent is for you to see this to the point of having the same experience as if it was you in the prodigal son story.

You might remember that my son finally came to his senses in realizing that he wanted to come back home – he, in no way was disappointed when he saw me running out to meet him in his filthy rags. The story is found in Luke 15.

Us: Oh, my, my – this is over the top stuff – I'm wondering why we couldn't have seen this on our own, I can only say, thank you, please give us more.

God: Okay then, let's go back to where you said you thought me to be angry over the breaking of my rules.

I know that's been a big misunderstanding, but I allowed that concept for a good reason. You might remember the story of Jonah as I demonstrated the results of 'scare tactic strategy' to win back many that would have never turned from evil any other way.

Us: Oh yes – I do remember the story – where the entire city turned from their wicked ways – but scare tactics – really?

God: Yes, I said scare tactics, something like you've used in the raising of your children; stop that, or I'll...

Us: Oh, I guess that does make sense – I doubt that we would have gotten their attention any other way.

We so appreciate this opportunity for conversation – so what's next, can you give us more?

God: Yes, the next one is about my rules, they have been misunderstood as legal rules with an imposed death penalty attached, which again, I allowed for good reason of demonstrating just how far the Devil would go with his evil strategies of deception.

Us: You mean to tell us that your rules are not legal? I've always thought they were – wow, we've been deceived.

God: Yes, I allowed it, but again, for good reason. But now that we're approaching the end of time, it's time to reveal one of my reasons for allowing you children to be deceived, not only about my rules, but many other things as well; for again, how better to demonstrate the Devil's ways than to allow him to deceive?

Through it all, I must bring you to the point of listening better. Remember, I made your world with a family setting, where you're, for sure, going to understand that your children rarely listen to you; does that ring a bell?

Us: Wow, does it ever!

God: Well then, you should know by now why I couldn't just tell you that the Devil was wrong, that he was spreading lies about me; after all, you are my children acting the same as your children – that of having a hard time listening to my words.

Although my methods may seem, somewhat unconventional, understand that I am the God that loves you unconditionally – willing to do whatever necessary, whatever it takes to win you back from the Devil's hold on you.

Us: Okay, that sounds good, and we're trying to listen, so hopefully you'll give us more.

God: Since you're asking for more, fasten your seat belts and hold on, the ride could get a little bumpy.

Us: Okay, consider it done, but what do you mean, a little bumpy?

God: I'm saying a little bumpy because I'm about to introduce you to some thoughts you're not accustomed to, which if you're listening, could be good news, some real good news that could change your whole outlook on life.

I've allowed the Devil to paint a distorted picture of who I am.

He has somehow, convinced you that you are in legal trouble for breaking my rules.

But it's not legal trouble you're in, instead, you have a listening, and trust problem. You've been listening to the Devil's view of me, trusting his words over the words from Jesus.

You have allowed yourselves to be deceived, even after I sent Jesus to enlighten you.

Like your own children, you don't listen very well, you tend to think of yourselves as rich and in need of nothing, which leads you to think you could never be deceived.

If the Devil was able to deceive about one third of the brilliant heavenly angles, as well as Adam and Eve – what makes you think you haven't been deceived as well?

Us: Oh, I think we're beginning to see something, is it that one of your main purposes for this world is to have the whole universe view the results of being deceived about you?

God: Now it's my turn to express excitement – I'm so proud of you – better late than never for listening; for this is exactly what I had recorded in 1st Corinthians 4:9.

You've been chosen to be on stage for everyone, as well as the angels, to view how crafty the Devil has been in leading you astray.

Many religions argue among each other that their beliefs are superior to others, which is the same spirit held within the heart of Lucifer before he was thrown out of Heaven.

This type of spirit feeds off being presented an improper picture of ME.

Hopefully eyes will be opened to see the downside of being superior to others and where it leads.

Us: Oh, what you're saying is so true, even in my own church we've been taught from childhood that we alone have the truth.

Now that you mention it, I see what you're saying about the arrogance of that type of spirit.

God: Yes, what I'm saying is that if you created would dwell more on the message Jesus came to reveal about ME - what I'm like – maybe you could even see that it could have been ME that washed a dozen pair of dirty feet, even the feet of the betrayer.

US: We must say your explanation on these issues has us speechless.

God: Okay then, back to talking more about my rules, you know the ten I wrote in stone, they're *instructive* rules about how you've been made to function – like I said, my rules are not legal in nature.

If my rules for living were legal, the enemy would come up with a way in which a high-powered attorney could get rule breakers **forgiven without a heart change.**

The Devil suggests that you must believe that Jesus paid your legal sin debt at the cross, simply believe, to gain forgiveness.

What's being missed is what keeps the rule breakers from breaking the rules over, and over again?

This concept is sure to turn the high-powered attorney into a hero for getting you forgiven repeatedly.

This concept may be okay for a time, but a time is coming for everyone to be off baby food and on to the solid food of godly principles, which can cause a heart change.

I sent Jesus to reveal this to you. However, the enemy has you so wrapped up in your own behavior that you don't seem to see it.

The way to see it and to become AT-ONE with us is to feed on the ways of Jesus, recorded throughout Matthew, Mark, Luke, and John.

It's about understanding that Jesus came with a message, the good news message about Me – that I'm not as the enemy has portrayed Me to be – that I'm just like Jesus, surely no one to be afraid of – for again, I love you all with an unconditional love.

Us: Oh, we just have to say it again, and again – this is outstanding good stuff God, this is so great, it's beyond words to express.

We so appreciate this, please, don't stop, give us more.

God: Okay, you asked for it – In the past you've been led to believe that rule breaking was the issue – that forgiveness from me was what you needed, but the truth is, you need to be healed from ingesting the poison of sin.

Here's an example: If a diesel fuel tank was accidentally filled with gasoline, upon starting the engine, it would surely cease to function because the diesel engine wasn't designed to handle gasoline.

But when you learn to discern the difference in realizing you made a big mistake, simply remember; I'm the Great Physician that's more than willing to heal the damage done.

In other words, to clean and repair your clogged up system; for those that come to me, I will never send away – found in John 6:37 last part.

Us: Well, what can we say, that surely makes more sense than anything we've heard before, it almost sounds too simple – please, tell us more.

God: Because you have the tendencies not to listen, I chose to take you through deep water, so to speak – so you could experience what it means to be deceived – seeing for yourselves the ways of the deceiving Devil; for how else am I going to get you humble enough to listen?

Some may have thought that the pain, suffering, and death is punishment for wrongdoing. However, it may be useful for the young to perceive it that way, to get their attention.

But for those that are ready for solid food, it's meant for demonstrating just how evil the Devil's ways are.

For the **universe** to be safe from the rise of evil ever happening again – all my created must be convinced, beyond any doubt that my ways are right - that my love for them is unconditional – that no sacrifice, not even the sacrifice of Jesus, was necessary, to gain My forgiveness. For Jesus went through it all to change you – not to change Me.

It's not enough for me to just say that I'm God, the Creator that loves you, but instead to achieve this type of understanding, I chose to send Jesus, my Son to demonstrate what unconditional love is, what it means.

Notice how the Devil has changed the entire emphasis to the plan of salvation – over to having hundreds of different groups arguing over how to be legally forgiven and saved?

The Devil's design was meant to take your attention off or away from getting to know Me, the real kind of God I am?

Us: Well, I guess you really did have a good reason for us to fasten our seat belts, because to think that the now taught plan of salvation is filled with a distorted picture of you, could be very bumpy for many.

Accepting that we've been deceived this way, is a hard pill to swallow, since many of us were taught spiritually twisted things from childhood.

God: Yes, tough love experiences are never easy, but sometimes necessary.

Since you were made with free will choice, it's totally necessary for ALL my created to own my ways of love for one another.

This is why it's said, "To know ME, is life eternal." But to really know me, only comes from spending time in feeding on the messages Jesus came to give.

Us: Wow God, we can now see why we've been confused, is because, with the many different Bible believing religions claiming their picture of you is the only correct one; which one were we to believe?

God: The quick answer to that, if there were a correct one, what do you suppose that would do to the ego of its members; would they think of themselves as superior, rich, and in need of nothing?

It's so necessary that ALL my created come to the place to understand that self-pride was at the core of Lucifer's fall.

But I do see you're beginning to understand some, because you really did bring up a very powerful question about who to believe or what to follow.

Your question leads ME to reveal just how sneaky and deceptive the Devil has been in twisting some of my words.

I've allowed this because you need to see that many of you have been led astray by not totally listening to the words of Jesus.

The truth about your Creator is found in the stories about Jesus, in how he treated, even his enemies.

I know this must be a big shocker, but what more can I say? The main reason behind sending Jesus to your world was to expose and straighten out the lies about ME that began with Lucifer while he was still in Heaven.

Jesus came to reveal the real ME, and to expose how the Devil had distorted my picture to the world.

Many of you, have thought the original text holds the truth, vs translations, but consider the Devils deceptive influence over the biblical writers from the beginning of time.

The Devil would like it to appear that every word in Scripture was dictated by ME – regardless of the many different writers and their interpretations.

His purpose was to lead people astray with added and twisted meanings to words.

Us: Oh my, this is over the top – If we can't trust in the authority of the Bible, what can trust?

God: I'm simply trying to reveal that words in any book can be distorted – but to actually witness the life of Jesus for yourself is how to see ME as I am.

By the time I sent Jesus to your world, the Devil had been roaming the earth for many years, distorting the picture of ME to the biblical scholars of the day.

You have the history of what happened as they nailed Jesus to the cross; have you any idea of why they did that – what was the real reason for their anger?

Us: Now that you mention it, I'm not sure we've thought about that because most of us have been taught to think about Jesus as taking our place in the death we deserve. Past that, at least for me, I was never drawn to wonder why they killed him.

God: The Devil thought he had the biblical scholars under his influence; they had the masses believing that I needed to be appeased with the blood of the most spotless animal available – a better sacrifice.

Consider the story of Jesus flipping over some tables within the temple because the leaders were scamming the people out of their money with the concept of them needing a better sacrifice.

And when the people brought their best animal – they were told it wasn't good enough, that they had to trade theirs for a better one, naturally costing the people up to their life savings.

But when Jesus came upon the scene exposing the falsities of this practice, it put them into a tailspin because it was, very quickly, becoming a threat to their flow of income as well as threating their power over the people.

The spiritual leaders had the masses of people believing in a fear-based gospel, with Me having to be appeased before I would grant them forgiveness.

And as you know, history is known to repeat itself – for the same fear-based teachings exists today.

The only difference is that the masses thought a Messiah was coming that would save them from the rigid Roman rulers.

But now, it's frequently taught that Jesus came, primarily, to die in your place, that the animal sacrifices were only to point forward to the BETTER BLOOD of Jesus to appease or satisfy MY allegedly taught, legal demands.

If you were really listening you could hear a hint of extortion in that concept, which is far from reality. For Jesus didn't die to satisfy ME, but instead he went through a horrible death to change you.

If all of you could see yourselves torturing and killing the one you have come to love, the concept is meant to sicken you deep within your emotions, enough to having you run from evil.

US: Oh my, what an enlightenment, what a difference to understand; how could we have missed this? It's so obvious, we have so much more to learn about the real YOU.

After YOU have explained this, I can't for the life of me, figure out how we, so-called, respectful people, could have pictured YOU as torturing, and putting to death those that refuse YOU, and calling it DEVINE JUSTICE?

God: Oh, I so enjoy your profound thinking. I now see that you may have been listening some.

Us: Yes, we're all hoping we now have it right, but correct me if I'm wrong.

What we've heard you say is that <u>the evil ways of the Devil are on stage for us to experience, and the whole universe to</u>

witness – giving all of us reason to run from evil.

The on-stage concept you gave us in 1st Corinthians 4 explains a lot for us - us having to go through the bad stuff of pain, suffering, and death, even as we attempt to tell the truth about you.

That text seems to explain how the Devil has worked within the spiritual realm of puffing many of us up in our so called, holiness, thinking of ourselves as superior, rich, and in need of nothing.

I especially like your question at the end, in 1st Corinthians 4:21 where you asked, what do we prefer?

What I'm hearing you ask, "What do we prefer? Shall I come to you with threatening words of a burning torturing Hell, or shall I come in love and with a gentle spirit – what would you prefer?

Wow! With gentleness, of course, the very picture of who YOU ARE?"

We're realizing you've revealed the ways of the Devil all along – thank you.

The very picture of YOU acting through the life of Jesus as he healed the people of their ills, is a direct opposite picture of YOU punishing people with pain, suffering, and death for breaking the rules.

We're beginning to see why <u>You've allowed the Devil to deceive us, was for us to become fortified against ever being taken-in or deceived again</u>, as some of the angels and Eve were.

Is that right, does it seem as if we are getting it?

God: Yes, I'm so impressed and proud of you to have come this far in understanding my main concerns, gives me hope that you're about ready to take the real good news gospel to the world.

Can you now see, if I were to simply tell you everything up front without you experiencing the Devil's ways for yourselves, would you have believed me?

Us: Oh, you are so right, what enlightenment YOU have given us; so much so, I think most of us are on overload. Maybe we should rest some to allow all this to soak in.

But we can't thank you enough - there are no words to express our gratitude – but to simply say, thank you, thank you, thank you!

< --- >

If the message within has soaked in, it should be time to think, don't you think – to think about what's currently being taught about God, versus what you have just experienced?

Shouldn't we have concern about what kind of KINGDOM we are to be saved in – meaning, what the KING is like?

A Short Summary

The Digest Version

This, in no way is meant to be a put-down to religions — for I believe God has allowed all the different spiritual beliefs for a purpose — it's part of God demonstration in preparing us or fortifying us against ever being deceived again throughout eternity.

< ---- >

When God's lead angel "Lucifer" - right within the heavenly control center, allowed his superiority to take him down the wrong road of thinking he could be a God — what was God to do but make a place for his evil intent to be exposed.

It may make sense that God took an existing planet and turn it into a place we now call earth — we might even want to call it the Devil's sandbox — so to speak.

At this point, I must make it clear about the strategy Lucifer used in his erroneous campaign to become the lead in Heaven.

*Like most political campaigns, he made evil accusations against God's character. Therefore, turning the **universal issue** into the trustworthiness of God.*

This is when war broke out in Heaven and Lucifer, now known as the Devil, was cast down to earth among the newly created family of Adam and Eve.

When the evil of his ways on earth reached the highest level, in demonstration, God destroyed all but eight people with the great flood.

The demo was to reveal that all the might and power to destroy evil would only be short lived – for when the world became repopulated, the people went back to the Devil's ways of evil.

God gave us another matching story in the book of Jonah. After the whole city of Nineveh was scared into turning their lives around, in the next generation the people, again, went back to the Devil's ways of evil.

After experiencing the evidence within this publication about what happened way back in biblical history – hopefully, you've caught the concept of the great deceiver putting the blame of bringing sin into the world on to Adam and Eve, instead of himself.

He simply deceived Eve into believing that God had lied to her – therefore, leading her into breaking the rules. (Gen.3:4)

At that point, the great deceiver was on his way to having everyone concerned into the belief that we are in legal trouble with God, along with the concept of God being angry over His rules being broken.

This is where the purpose of sacrifice was introduced, as a way to appease the wrath of any, and all gods (deities).

Biblical history reveals that before Jesus came to earth, this concept of having to appease their gods with a blood sacrifice to gain forgiveness, was alive and well.

In fact, the Devil had so distorted the peoples' beliefs about God, he had some into the horrifying practice of sacrificing their own children in the process of satisfying their angry gods.

Now, with all due respect for the religions of the world, with the Devil's ways in control, is it any wonder that the now taught plan of salvation (2022) is into the belief that God the Father needed to be appeased with the better blood sacrifice of Jesus, before He was willing to forgive?

Something has to be horribly wrong here, when the religions of the world are refusing to listen to Revelation 12 where it states that the Devil will lead the whole world astray. Being led astray about what God is like.

The issues here are not over how to be forgiven or even over the difference between good and evil – but with the solid rock evidence within this publication, it should speak loud and clear, that the universal issue is over *the trustworthiness of God, the kind of God He is.*

For what kind of God would demand a blood sacrifice of appeasement before granting forgiveness? *(Surely the Devil's conjured-up view)*

It's simply, that the whole world of religions has been led astray, just as Revelation 12 describes - by believing that every word in Scripture is God breathed – when it's NOT. (Look back to page 46)

This has led the whole world of religion into mass confusion over the character of God – leading biblical scholars, the world over, into many complicated ways in how to gain God's forgiveness.

But as said before, forgiveness is not the issue – but instead, knowing God is the issue, the way to eternal life.   (John 17:3)

Unfortunately, the Devil has most convinced that it's all about Jesus, in what he has done for us, in getting us past an angry god.

Just in case you didn't know, it's taught the world over, that Jesus became the better sacrifice to calm the wrath of an offended God – along with - that God the Father has accepted the sacrifice of Jesus in our behalf.

It's said, if we believe this, that our salvation is accomplished in the person and work of Jesus. It's also said that this is the good news within the gospel – just believe it!

But, if you could be setting at the feet of Jesus, LISTENING, you would quickly discover that Jesus did not support this.

The Devil has people believing, by way of assuming – just say it enough times, over and over, and the masses of people will assume it to be true.

People, the world over, have assumed that God is angry over our sinning and have just assumed He needed to be appeased *(as a heathen god)* with the precious blood of Jesus before He will calm down enough to forgive us.

They have just assumed that the cross of Calvary is where our sins were terminated, by Jesus dying in our place.

But I'm here to tell you, this is the Devil's conjured-up picture of God, making God out to be what He is NOT.

At the cross of Calvary, Jesus dying for us, was absolutely necessary – it was necessary to change you and me, not the Father.

The truth of this is found within the question and history of **why** and **how** Jesus died.

Question: Why did Jesus die on the cross, was it really to appease the Father's anger, or to change the heart of you and me, after realizing what we have done?

History reveals that it was you and I – the most spiritual people of the day, that crucified Jesus.

Of course, the Devil wants to cover that up with the *LIE* that God the Father killed Jesus in our place, as our substitute to appease His wrath against sin. *(Along with satisfying the, allegedly taught, legal demands of God's laws.)*

But again, I don't hear Jesus supporting that.

Instead, evidence supports that the whole sacrificial system of the animals as well as the sacrifice of Jesus was designed to sicken the heart of the person administering the act.

For God is concerned that we see the evil we have done, with a desire to have a heart change – just as David did, as stated in Psalms 51: "Create in me a pure heart, O God, and renew a steadfast spirit within me."

It's the Devil that says God needed to be appeased before He would forgive.

But with Jesus demonstrating the ways of God, it should be seen that God is our Great Physician more than ready to heal the damage we have done to ourselves.

Again, something has to be horribly wrong in what is being taught throughout the world about God.

Mainly because Jesus said in John 14 that if you have seen me, you have seen the Father. Also, in John 16:26 Jesus said he did *NOT* have to plead the Father in our behalf, because the Father loves us the same as he does.

Are you sure you know God –

the God that Jesus came to reveal?

John 17:3 – *To know God is life eternal.*

To know the true God that Jesus came to reveal, is to know perfect freedom away from the many avenues of deception that has led the whole world into wandering -

"WHY - If there is a loving God, then why all the pain, suffering, and death?"

It's recorded in John 17:21 that Jesus was praying that we would all become AT-ONE with them (Jesus and his Father) as they are AT-ONE with each other.

Are you listening to Jesus?

(Borrowed)

'*The Devil sought to intercept every ray of light from God. He sought to cast his shadow across the earth, that men might lose the true view of God's character, and that the knowledge of God might become extinct in the earth.*

He had caused truth of vital importance to be so mingled with error that it had lost its significance.

God's laws have been so burdened with needless exactions and tradition, its caused the picture of God to be represented as exacting, revengeful, unforgiving, and severe.

But Jesus came to teach the truth about his Father, to correctly represent Him to us.'

This is the recorded picture of Christ's mission, found in both Luke 4:43 & John 17:4-6.

It's also been said – *'that the whole purpose, yes, the whole purpose for the mission of Jesus to earth was to set and keep us right by revealing the truth about our most gracious heavenly Father.*

It really could be time to think

don't you think?

Hosea 11 (Paraphrased)

"It was I who taught you to walk – It was I who healed you – I led you with cords of kindness, with ties of love, and I bent down to feed you.

But you still are determined to turn from me.

Oh, how can I give you up, how can I let you go, my heart winces within; my compassion grows warm and tender. <u>I won't act on the heat of anger</u>, for I am God and not a human being."

John 14 - (Paraphrased)

"Let not your heart be troubled: Trust in God. Trust also in me. In my Father house are many rooms; if it were not so, I would have told you. I'm going to prepare a place for you, and I will be back to take you **home** with me, that where I am, there you may be also."

Are you listening?

This world is not our home!

By the way, I hope to see you there, I mean throughout eternity – you know, the place some of us call Heaven!

God has surely given us enough evidence on what He is like – but maybe we've been in our comfort zones and asleep, as described in another book –

"The Midnight Cry"

The message of Matthew 25

You know, the five wise & the five foolish.

For more spiritual straight talk on what God is like, you're invited to view what the thief saw as he hung on a cross, next to Jesus.

It caused him to think,

"Wow! If this is what God is like,

then count me in!"

At the bottom line

there is no vengeance in the heart of God.

As you have learned within this publication, Jesus came primarily to reveal God to us.

The **huge alert** is here and now - based on the condition of the world, it would be great if all teachers and preachers could get on board with Matthew 24:14 – when 'the gospel of the kingdom' *(the good news about the kind of person God is – the same message Jesus came to proclaim)* is taken to the world – THEN THE END WILL COME!!!

So, what's holding us back — are we afraid of losing our flow of income – are we afraid we'll lose power over the masses of people?

Are we allowing history to repeat itself?

Come on, **Y-All**, it's time to work on putting an end to all the pain, suffering, and death.

Highly recommended

Download the audio versions of:

"Are We Sure We Know God?"

"A Reality Check or What?"

Paper backs

"An Awakening?"

"The Ultimate Rest of the Story"

"The Midnight Cry"

"Wow! if this is what God is like, then count me in"

"The Gig is up / The Charade is Over"

and a few more

Found at: TimeToThink.us

Click on "View Books"

Written by Edward Sager, founder of TimeToThink.us

Made in the USA
Monee, IL
28 April 2022